The Amazing Book of SCIENCE EXPERIMENTS

CONTENTS

Materials

This book reveals important ideas about science through a variety of simple experiments. You can perform these easily yourself, at home, without any special scientific equipment. In this first section, you'll investigate materials science. This is the study of the chemical properties of matter. That includes matter in its various forms—solid, liquid, and gas.

Unfolding secrets

Materials come in all shapes, sizes, states, and temperatures. When you start thinking of materials, you're thinking of the world itself. Whether you're observing an iceberg breaking off the Antarctic coast, a glass falling to the floor and smashing, or an ice cream melting and dripping down your hand, you're learning about materials and how they behave.

The experiments in the following pages will take you into a world where materials bend, break, melt, expand, contract, and sometimes behave in ways that may at first seem confusing. By the end of the chapter you'll see how everyday materials hide some real mysteries—and how mysterious objects might turn out to be familiar.

Invisible Gases

Most gases are invisible, but we can still observe some of their properties and how they behave. A relatively dense and heavy gas, for example, will sink through a lighter one, just as a heavier liquid sinks through a lighter liquid. Try this simple experiment on a bright, sunny day in front of a light or white wall that faces the sun.

1

On a table by the wall, assemble baking soda (sometimes called baking powder), vinegar, a big glass container, a tablespoon, and a wooden spoon.

2

Pour 200 ml (1 cup) of vinegar into the container.

3

Add 2 tablespoons of baking soda to the vinegar and stir with the wooden spoon.

4

Hold the container out so that its shadow is visible on the wall behind you.

5

Slowly tip the container, taking care that none of the liquid pours out.

6

You should see the shadow of the gas pouring out.

YOU WILL NEED: baking soda | vinegar | glass container | a tablespoon | a wooden spoon

HOW DOES IT WORK?

When you mix the baking soda with vinegar in the glass container, it triggers a chemical reaction that produces a gas called carbon dioxide. That gas is denser and heavier than air, so it can be "poured" just as a liquid could be poured.

Unlike air, the denser carbon dioxide gas casts a shadow. It's that shadow of the heavy gas that you see being poured from the container.

Natural gas flows out from oil wells as oil is extracted. Unlike carbon dioxide, the dispersing gas is lighter than air, so it rises.

Natural gas is normally invisible, but it burns brightly once oil engineers disperse it by lighting it.

Metal Mysteries

We think of metals as strong, unbending construction materials. But not all metals are alike—for example, mercury is a liquid at room temperature. And even the most solid metals can surprise us. It's all due to the movement of the molecules that make them up. See for yourself with this experiment.

1 Tighten the lids of both jars so that it would be hard to unscrew them.

2 Hold one of the jars in the sink and run cold water over it.

3 Continue holding it there for 30 seconds and try to unscrew it. It will still feel stiff.

4 Repeat the steps with the second jar, this time running water that's hot (but not too hot to touch).

5 Try to unscrew its lid; you should find it much easier.

YOU WILL NEED: two identical jam jars with metal lids | hot and cold water

The steel used for roller coaster rails is strong, but, like the lid of the jar held under hot water, it still expands when heated.

In extremely hot weather, the side-to-side movement of a heavy train can make the expanded rails bend. It's all because of the mysterious workings of molecules.

HOW DOES IT WORK?

The experiment with the glass jars demonstrates how the metal lid expands when it is warmed. Scientists call this thermal expansion. It happens when the heated molecules in the metal begin to move farther apart. The result is that the metal gets slightly bigger.

The glass jar also expands, but much less than the metal. That means that the metal lid "outgrows" the jar and becomes a little bit looser.

Changing States

Cooking is a domestic science and this experiment helps you understand why—heating and cooling a material causes the particles to act differently, changing its state. Here, the chocolate changes from a solid to a liquid state and back again. Make sure to ask an adult to help with the boiling water.

1 Rinse the rose leaves and dry them with a paper towel. Pat them lightly as they rest on a paper towel.

2 Half-fill the saucepan with water and ask an adult to warm it.

3 Break up the chocolate into small pieces and put them in the mixing bowl.

4 Ask the adult to put the bowl on top of the pan. When it's melted, ask the adult to give you the bowl.

5 Use the melted chocolate to "paint" the rose leaves and leave them to cool.

6 Now, remove the leaves to reveal an imprinted leaf pattern.

YOU WILL NEED: 5 rose leaves | paper towel | water | a saucepan | a mixing bowl | a bar of chocolate | a clean paintbrush

Materials have different freezing points. Chocolate is solid at room temperature, but water is a liquid. Here, the water dripping from a warm roof freezes in the sub-freezing air at the edge, creating solid icicles.

The weak winter sun isn't warm enough to melt the icicles, so they remain hanging in their frozen, solid state.

HOW DOES IT WORK?

In the cooking experiment, the molecules inside the chocolate are tightly packed, keeping it solid at room temperature. As the chocolate warms, those molecules begin to move more quickly and farther apart. When the chocolate melts, it changes into a liquid state. This process is used to shape chocolate into bars, buttons, and even figures.

Forces

Scientists describe a force as strength or energy to cause or change movement. When someone gives you a push on your bike, they're applying force. You might then brake, applying the force of friction, to slow down to prevent falling, which is caused by another force—gravity.

Strength and Energy

Think of some of the more familiar forces that involve pushing or pulling—picking up a heavy shopping bag, being pulled along when you're out walking your dog, or pushing a lawn mower. They're all examples of forces at work, and it's easy to see or feel their effects. With a bit of exploring, and experiments, you can discover some fascinating secrets about forces.

For example, did you know that water and even air can provide a powerful force? Or that you can change a force with tricks of time or space? The following pages will help you see forces can cause or change movement in some surprising ways.

Air Force

Gases can generate or change powerful forces. But you can see some of those forces in action with a familiar gas that's always around you—air. This simple experiment with an air current from a blow-dryer and a table tennis ball can help demonstrate how huge aircraft can fly without falling out of the sky.

1 Turn the blow-dryer to the coolest level. This experiment depends on moving air, not heat.

2 Point the blow-dryer up, holding the ball in your other hand and turn it on.

3 Slowly move the ball toward the upward-flowing air, approaching the dryer from above.

4 Release the ball when you feel it begin to move in your hand.

5 The ball will float just where you let it go.

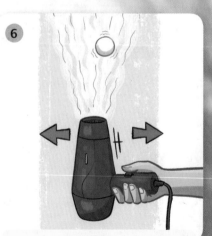

6 See what happens if you move the blow-dryer from side to side.

YOU WILL NEED: a blow-dryer (ask permission before you borrow it) | a table tennis ball

Warming air rises, like a tunnel of air rushing from the blow-dryer. We call the upward currents, "thermals." An eagle uses thermals to glide for long periods.

Broad wings catch as much wind as possible.

HOW DOES IT WORK?

The table tennis ball experiment depends on Bernoulli's principle, which states that a gas exerts less pressure (pushes less hard) as it moves faster. Air presses in every direction, so the air rushing out of the blow-dryer is like a tunnel of weak pressure surrounded by higher pressure.

The rushing air pushes up the table tennis ball, but farther away is air that is still, and this pushes on the current of moving air. Even if you tilt the blow-dryer, the ball will still float, held inside its "tunnel" by the still air around it.

Momentum in Action

Momentum always involves force, as well as mass and velocity (speed and direction). The combined momentum of two objects is conserved after they collide. So, the total momentum remains the same, but it can be transferred from one object to another. Try this easy experiment to show conservation of momentum in action.

1 Hold a basketball or volleyball at arm's length and drop it on to a hard surface outside.

2 Note how high the basketball bounces.

3 Do the same with a tennis ball.

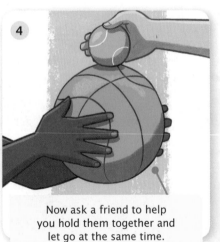

4 Now ask a friend to help you hold them together and let go at the same time.

5 The tennis ball will bounce much higher than either ball did before.

YOU WILL NEED: a basketball/volleyball | a tennis ball | a volunteer

HOW DOES IT WORK?

This experiment demonstrates conservation of momentum. That simply means that when two objects collide, their combined momentum remains the same. However, some of the momentum might be lost from one object (the basketball in this case) and transferred to another (the tennis ball). So when the balls are dropped together—and collide—the tennis ball receives extra momentum that sends it sky-high.

Carnival rides help turn conservation of momentum into boundless fun.

"Bumper cars" offer constant demonstrations of this effect as they collide and bounce off one another.

Resistant Friction

We encounter friction all around us every day. It's the force that acts between two objects that are in contact, and it resists movement. As with other forces, a small amount goes unnoticed. But if it builds, then it's hard to ignore. Even the pages of books can be locked together using no more than the force of friction, as this simple experiment shows.

1

Rest the two books beside each other on a table with the spines pointing out.

2

Peel back most of the pages of each book.

3

Feed the pages over each other a few pages a time so they overlap about halfway.

4

Continue in this way until you reach the front.

5

Ask a friend to pull the books apart—they will be stuck.

When the cyclist brakes, friction from the brake rubber resists the wheel's rotation and slows the bike down.

YOU WILL NEED: 2 paperback books

HOW DOES IT WORK?

The books in your experiment stick together due to the force of friction, which resists the movement of the pages sliding against each other.

Each overlay of pages creates a small amount of friction, which you can feel if you slide the pages back and forth. Every overlay adds another small bit of force, then another, and so on. Eventually there is such a build-up of friction that the books are locked together.

Racing sports rely on friction to safely control speed. Some turns on hillside trails are too tight for BMX racers to take fast—they must slow down.

Light and Sound

We use two of our senses—sight and hearing—to help us make sense of our surroundings. Some of the most interesting experiments involve light and sound. They both travel through space in waves, and understanding this wave motion unlocks some of the secrets of these forms of energy.

Solving mysteries

Scientists can measure the distance between these waves (or wavelength) as well as how many times they vibrate in a single second (their frequency). Whatever we see or hear are the results of those energy wavelengths and frequencies, making things change their shade or pitch.

Both sound and light waves can "bend" or be reflected along the way as they hit or pass through some materials. Those changed paths can also lead to light and sound becoming focused, making them particularly powerful within a relatively small area. What we see or hear also depends on whether the source of the light or sound is heading toward or away from us. These distortions can be confusing, making people question the evidence of their senses. The following experiments aim to answer those questions while prompting you to think of questions of your own.

The Sound of Music

Even if we don't realize it, we use science—and mathematics—to appreciate our best-loved songs and melodies. You can even demonstrate this connection between science and music with an easy experiment to create sound waves, complete with a makeshift musical instrument, at home.

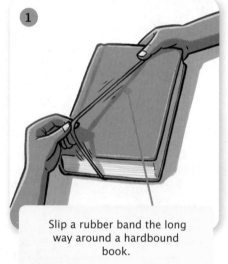

1 Slip a rubber band the long way around a hardbound book.

2 Slide the two pencils under the loop near the ends of the book.

Like the strings on musical instruments, vocal cords in our throat vibrate to make different sounds.

3 Pluck the band (now slightly raised) and listen to the musical note.

4 Press your finger down firmly halfway along the band.

5 Pluck again and listen to the different tone.

YOU WILL NEED: a hardback book | a rubber band | 2 pencils

A microphone amplifies a singer's voice. It makes it sound stronger, but it doesn't change the notes that she sings.

HOW DOES IT WORK?

The rubber band in your experiment vibrates like a guitar string. When you shorten the string by half its length (Step 4) and pluck the band either side, it sounds like the same note, but higher. In fact, it's an octave higher. If you called the first note "Do," and then sang up the scale, through "Re," "Mi," and so on, the second note would be a higher "Do." The sound waves vibrate twice as fast (we hear it as one octave higher) when the band is half is long.

How to Bend Light

Light will travel in a straight path—like the Sun's light reaching Earth—unless it hits something to change that path. One result is reflection, or bouncing off an object. But other, stranger, effects can occur as light passes through some substances. The light can then change direction, or refract, as it continues on its path. You'll need a darkened room to show off your light-bending skill in this experiment.

1 Cut a slit about 0.2in (0.5cm) wide and 2in (5cm) high in a narrow end of the shoebox.

2 Fill the bottle with water and screw the cap on.

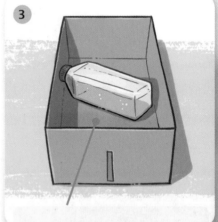

3 Angle the bottle on its side in the shoebox.

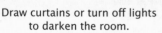

4 Draw curtains or turn off lights to darken the room.

5 Shine a light through the slot.

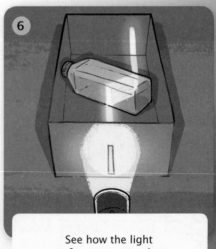

6 See how the light refracts at an angle.

YOU WILL NEED: a cardboard box | scissors | a clear water bottle with flat sides | water | a flashlight

Here's some dramatic evidence that light can bend (or refract) as it travels. Whether it does—and by how much—depends on the material that it passes through. This experiment shows how the beam of light is redirected, or refracted, as it passes through the water in the bottle.

By keeping the room dark, and the beam of light below the top of the shoebox, you make that bending path much easier to see.

The water in the bottle acts like a prism, an angled piece of clear material that refracts light.

A prism can also break down light into its different shades, just like in a rainbow.

Heat and Cold

Changes in temperature go to the heart of how all matter behaves—from the atomic level right up to the global. For example, the advance or retreat of the polar ice caps—a global effect with important consequences—depends on how much tiny water molecules move around at a minute level.

Change and movement

Heat is a form of energy that is transferred from one object to another. A hot oven, for example, transfers heat into a cake tin with liquid batter. That transfer warms the batter until it becomes a cake. A room becomes colder in winter when a window is opened, allowing heat to escape outside.

Heat energy is the result of the movement of the tiniest bits of matter—atoms, ions, and molecules—inside liquids, solids, or gases. That energy can flow from one substance to another because of a difference in temperature. So the scientists would say that "heat" is the transfer of "heat energy."

Cold is simply the absence of heat, so when we think that something has become cold, what has really happened is that it has lost heat. Heat transfer takes place constantly—from the changing weather to powering factories, to a melting ice-cream cone.

Heat Absorption

Heat is the transfer of a form of energy. How that heat energy is absorbed by (flows into and through) materials differs. It's also linked to how fast heat flows from a substance. We can notice it in large bodies of water. As summer approaches, the air absorbs heat quickly and becomes warm, but water is slower to absorb and remains chilly. Conversely, at the end of the summer, when ocean or lake water is still comfortable for swimming, the air has become colder. Pop a balloon to show how air absorbs heat faster than water.

1 Blow up an ordinary party balloon and tie it shut. It will be your "air balloon."

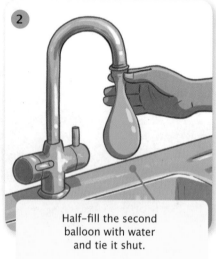

2 Half-fill the second balloon with water and tie it shut.

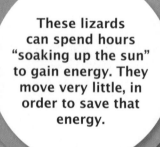

These lizards can spend hours "soaking up the sun" to gain energy. They move very little, in order to save that energy.

3 Set a lit candle in the bottom of the sink.

4 Hold the "air balloon" by the flame until it bursts.

5 Then try with the water balloon—it won't burst no matter how close it is.

YOU WILL NEED: 2 balloons | water | a candle

Heat from the candle quickly raises the air temperature enough to burst the first balloon. Water inside the second balloon and nearest the flame also warms up, but it rises away and is replaced by cooler water. That keeps the balloon safely below "bursting temperature."

Make sure that the candle is closest to the bottom of the balloon, so that the water can rise more easily. That will increase your chances of success.

Reptiles bask in the heat of the sun to warm their blood. Mammals, on the other hand, can regulate their own temperatures.

Balloon Boost

Your kitchen can become a testing lab to observe the effect of heat on a gas. Particles inside any heated substance move around more, and if possible, take up more space. And if the same number of particles take up more space, then the gas becomes less dense (since density refers to how much matter a particular volume contains). Less dense fluids and gases usually rise through denser ones, which is why warm air rises. The only scientific tools you'll need here are a freezer and the ceiling—and some helium balloons!

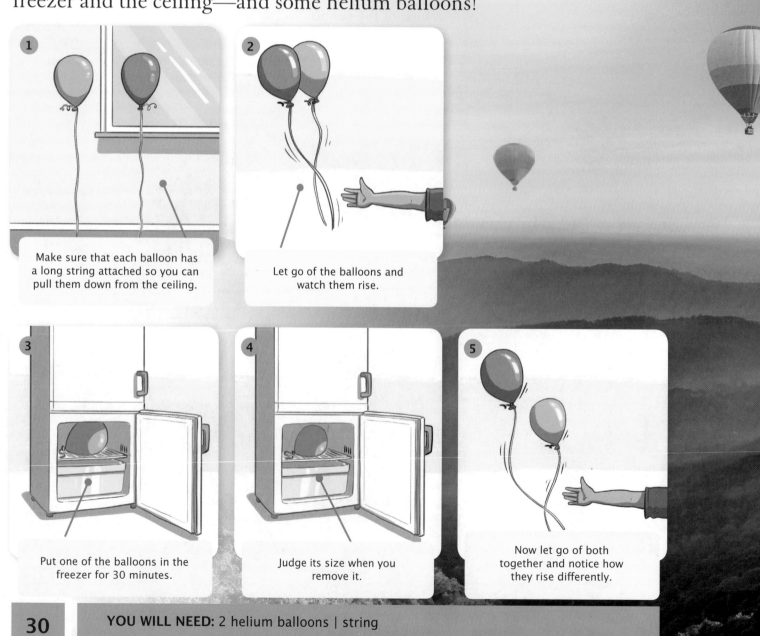

1. Make sure that each balloon has a long string attached so you can pull them down from the ceiling.

2. Let go of the balloons and watch them rise.

3. Put one of the balloons in the freezer for 30 minutes.

4. Judge its size when you remove it.

5. Now let go of both together and notice how they rise differently.

YOU WILL NEED: 2 helium balloons | string

Unlike your helium balloons, hot–air balloons contain ordinary air, so they need to be heated up before they can float up in the sky.

Warming the air inside the balloon makes it less dense, and lighter, than the surrounding air, giving it lift.

HOW DOES IT WORK?

Heat is the movement of particles in a substance, and in your experiment that substance is the helium gas inside the balloon. At room temperature, the helium is less dense than the air outside the balloon—so the balloon floats. Once it has been cooled, the helium particles move more slowly and take up less room inside it. Slower-moving helium molecules take up less space (the balloon shrinks a bit), and the helium becomes denser, so the balloon doesn't float so high.

The Freezing Point

Every substance has a freezing point, when it goes from a liquid state into a solid state. Most of us know the temperatures at which water usually changes state: it is ice (solid) up to 32°F (0°C), then liquid, and at 212°F (100°C) it becomes steam (gas). But adding other substances to water can alter the temperature of the phase changes.

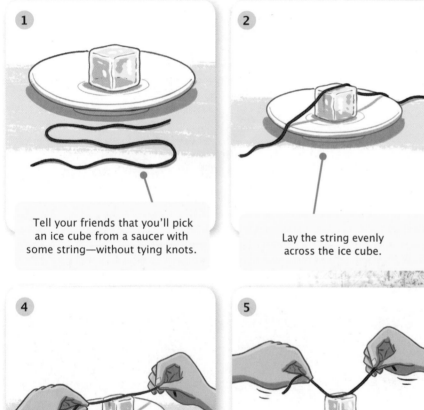

1 Tell your friends that you'll pick an ice cube from a saucer with some string—without tying knots.

2 Lay the string evenly across the ice cube.

3 Sprinkle salt over the ice cube, especially over the string lying on it.

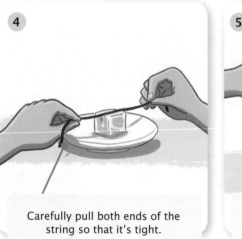

4 Carefully pull both ends of the string so that it's tight.

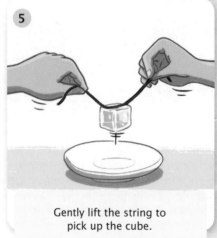

5 Gently lift the string to pick up the cube.

The truck pushes aside snow and ice to clear the road surface ready for the sprinkled salt.

YOU WILL NEED: an ice cube | a plate | string | salt

Snow-removal trucks sprinkle salt on roads to melt the ice so it is safer to drive.

HOW DOES IT WORK?

Salt water freezes at a slightly lower temperature than pure water. When you sprinkle salt onto the ice cube, it melts some of the ice near it, causing the string to rest in a watery gully. But as more ice melts, the salt solution becomes more dilute—and the freezing point creeps up again.

Eventually the water refreezes over the string. This means that you can lift the ice cube thanks to the frozen-in string.

Electricity and Magnetism

For centuries people believed that certain stones had magical properties to attract other materials and that lightning was a sign that the gods were angry. Now we know that those stones carry a magnetic charge and that lightning is a form of electricity—but they can still feel uncanny!

Opposites Attract

Both electricity and magnetism involve "opposites attracting." Electricity depends on the attraction between negatively charged particles called electrons and positively charged protons. Magnetic force can attract or repel objects, with magnetic fields having "poles" of attraction at opposite sides.

When scientists began to understand the basics of electricity and magnetism several hundred years ago, they viewed them as separate. We now know that they are part of a wider form of energy called electromagnetism. With that knowledge, engineers have been able to build powerful magnets powered by equally powerful electric forces.

Striking Static

Electricity is caused by the flow of electrons (negatively charged particles). Electron flow, called a current, is driven by the attraction of electrons to positively charged protons. In this way, electricity flows from a battery to power a TV remote, or from a wall outlet to switch on a toaster. But the word "static" means "not moving," so static electricity describes a build-up of a charge (positive or negative) that is not flowing. Static electricity is remarkably powerful, as this striking magic trick demonstrates.

1. Fill the bowl just over halfway with cereal, making sure that it's not tightly packed.

2. Briskly rub the plastic spoon with the woolly hat.

3. Wave the spoon slowly, about 15in (40cm) over the bowl.

4. Lower the spoon so that it's 2in (5cm) above the bowl.

5. You will see pieces of cereal start jumping up to the spoon.

YOU WILL NEED puffed rice cereal | a cereal bowl | a plastic spoon | a woolen hat or mitten

Lightning is an extremely powerful form of static electricity, with a massive build-up of negatively charged particles inside clouds.

The negative charge is attracted to positively charged objects below … and the lightning strikes.

HOW DOES IT WORK?

When you rub the plastic spoon with wool, you generate a negative charge on the spoon's surface. The build-up of this static charge then makes the cereal jump up to the spoon. Opposite charges attract, so positive charges build up on the cereal puffs closest to the spoon, and they jump up. But the charges weaken when the cereal hits the spoon, causing the pieces to become neutral and fall back down.

Magnetic Attraction

Gravity and magnetism can sometimes work against each other. The force of gravity pulls objects to other objects of greater mass. On Earth, the mass of the planet itself exerts that force. But a strong enough magnetic field can draw—or repel—objects in the opposite direction to the pull of gravity. Stage your own contest between magnetism and gravity in this experiment, and watch magnetism come out on top.

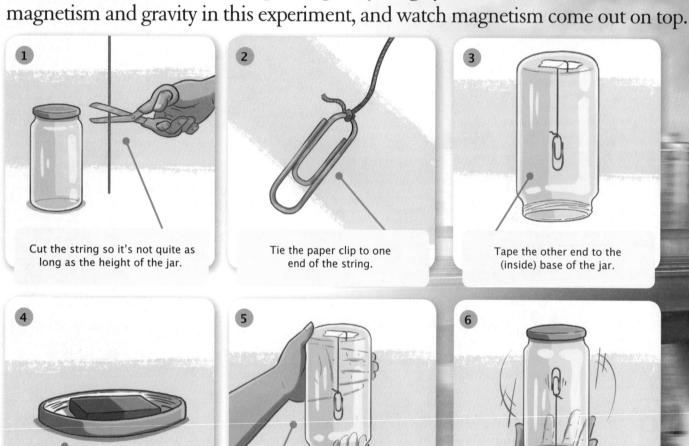

1 Cut the string so it's not quite as long as the height of the jar.

2 Tie the paper clip to one end of the string.

3 Tape the other end to the (inside) base of the jar.

4 Glue or tape the magnet to the inside of the lid and then close it.

5 Hold the jar upside-down so the paper clip hangs down.

6 Then turn the jar the right way round, and see what happens.

YOU WILL NEED: string | scissors | a jam jar | a paper clip | tape or glue | a bar magnet

The paper clip is pulled in opposite directions by two different forces. Normally, gravity would pull the clip down, just as anything dropped will fall toward the mass of the Earth. But the magnetic field created by the bar magnet was strong enough to overcome the force of gravity. Of course, that field would be weaker and unable to overcome gravity if the clip were farther away from it. But much more powerful magnetic fields can defy gravity by attracting—or repelling—massive objects.

Like the floating paperclip, Magnetic Levitation (MagLev) trains use magnetism to resist gravity.

The train glides above its tracks because a magnetized coil on the track repels a magnet on the underside of the train.

Dynamic Electromagnetism

An electromagnet is produced when electricity and magnetism work together—an electrical current running through a coil creates a magnetic field. The strength of the electromagnet depends on the strength of the current. Ask an adult to help with this experiment, and see how many paper clips a home-made electromagnet can pick up.

1 Ask an adult to use the wire cutters to snip a 20in (50cm) length of wire.

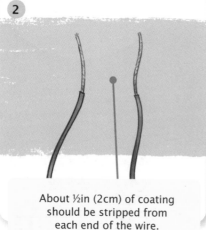

2 About ½in (2cm) of coating should be stripped from each end of the wire.

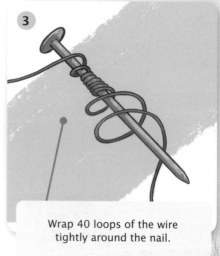

3 Wrap 40 loops of the wire tightly around the nail.

4 Make sure to leave both ends jutting out.

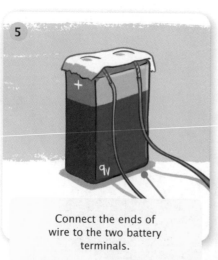

5 Connect the ends of wire to the two battery terminals.

6 Move one end of the nail close to a pile of paper clips and watch what happens.

YOU WILL NEED: insulated wire | wire cutters | a small iron nail | a 9–volt battery | paper clips

On a much larger scale than your simple coiled wire, scrapyards use powerful electromagnets to lift heavy metal objects.

Electromagnets can also sift through and separate magnetic metals (which contain iron and can be lifted) from nonmagnetic metals and other things.

HOW DOES IT WORK?

Your simple coiled wire becomes an electromagnet once it's connected—and the iron core (the nail) becomes magnetic enough to pick up several paper clips at once. The current flows along the wire in a circuit from one battery terminal to the other. As it passes through the coiled section of wire, a magnetic field is created inside the coil. Your electromagnet relies on electricity, and it will lose its magnetic power when either end of the wire is disconnected.

Living Things

One of the most basic divisions in scientific classification is between living and nonliving things. It's easy to identify some things—such as rocks or seawater—as nonliving. Similarly, no one would mistake a lion, oak tree, or human being for anything other than a living thing.

Shared Qualities

Classification can become a little more confusing, though, when we try to look at everything around us. We can say that all plants and animals are living things, but the category extends much further. Tiny bacteria, mushrooms, and even yeast are also living things.

Scientists define living things as having a number of shared qualities. These include the ability to grow, reproduce, regulate their own systems, and to react to stimuli (actions) around them. As well as these shared characteristics, many living things have developed special qualities of their own. The following pages will shed light on some of those fascinating features.

Finding the Light

Light and water are essential for photosynthesis, the chemical process that plants use to produce their own food. Because they need light to survive, plants can be surprisingly active in reacting to it. They grow—and sometimes move during the day—to increase their exposure to it. Plants can even turn corners in their search for light. See for yourself with this clever experiment.

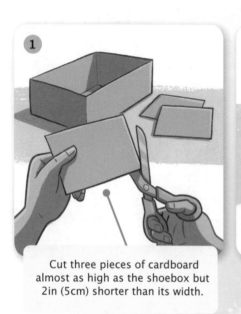

1 Cut three pieces of cardboard almost as high as the shoebox but 2in (5cm) shorter than its width.

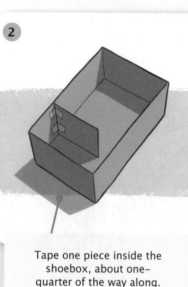

2 Tape one piece inside the shoebox, about one-quarter of the way along.

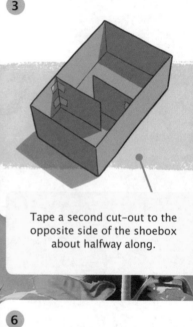

3 Tape a second cut-out to the opposite side of the shoebox about halfway along.

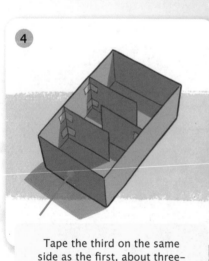

4 Tape the third on the same side as the first, about three-quarters of the way along.

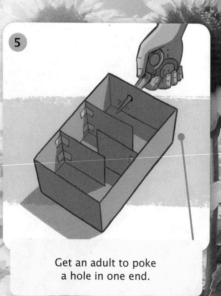

5 Get an adult to poke a hole in one end.

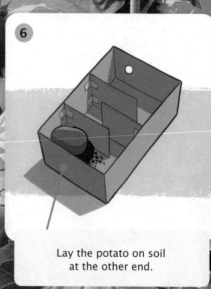

6 Lay the potato on soil at the other end.

YOU WILL NEED: a shoebox | cardboard | scissors | tape | potting soil | a sprouting potato

This experiment is an excellent demonstration of phototropism. That's the movement or growth of plants in response to light. Because light is so important to plant food production, plants seek it out. Auxin, the chemical that encourages cell growth, becomes concentrated on the side of the plant stem farther from the light. The stem grows faster on that side, helping the plant turn corners as it reacts to the light. In this case, the plant sensed the light coming from each tiny hatch.

Like the sprouting potato, other plants respond to light, too. Sunflowers live up to their name by the way they grow.

Growing sunflowers face the sun and slowly turn each day as they follow its course.

7

Cover the shoebox and place it near a light source.

8

Check every few days but cover again each time.

Proof of Life

All living organisms need nutrition in order to grow and stay healthy. Most nutrients are combined with other substances, so organisms need to break down (digest) those substances to nourish themselves. Digestion is a chemical process and the material that isn't used for food is discharged as waste. And that waste, in turn, might nourish other organisms. Different living organisms produce different kinds of waste, and this experiment uses one kind to blow up a balloon!

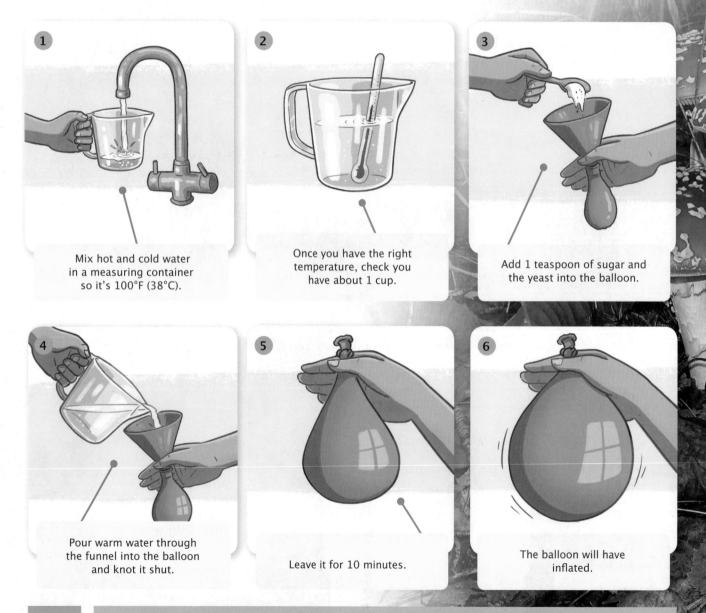

1 Mix hot and cold water in a measuring container so it's 100°F (38°C).

2 Once you have the right temperature, check you have about 1 cup.

3 Add 1 teaspoon of sugar and the yeast into the balloon.

4 Pour warm water through the funnel into the balloon and knot it shut.

5 Leave it for 10 minutes.

6 The balloon will have inflated.

YOU WILL NEED: a measuring container | water | a thermometer | sugar | a teaspoon | a packet of yeast | a balloon | a funnel

Yeasts and mushrooms, like these toxic toadstools, are all fungi. Mushrooms get most of their nutrition from the decayed bits of vegetation.

Like other fungi, toadstools don't need light to make food and grow, because they are not plants.

HOW DOES IT WORK?

Yeast is a living organism, and a relative of mushrooms. This experiment creates the conditions for yeast to be nourished and to digest food. The warm water made it easier for the yeast to absorb and digest the sugar (its food).

Just as animals burp while digesting food, the yeast also gives off a gas (in this case carbon dioxide) while it digests the food. And that's what fills the balloon.

Glossary

ABSORB
To take in or soak up through chemical or physical action.

AMPLIFY
To increase the strength of energy that travels in waves.

CHARGE
A measure of the flow of electrons, either positive or negative.

CIRCUIT
The closed path that an electrical current follows.

CONDUCTOR
A material that allows energy to flow through it.

CONTRACT
Become smaller.

CURRENT
The rate of flow of an electrical charge past a certain point.

DECAY
To rot or deteriorate, usually because of the action of bacteria or microscopic organisms.

DENSITY
The amount of mass contained in a specific volume of a substance.

DIGEST
To break down a substance into the parts that make it up.

ELECTROMAGNETIC
A type of energy that can take many forms and which operates in tandem with magnetic forces.

ELECTRON
A negatively charged particle that forms part of an atom.

EXPAND
To occupy more space.

FORCE
Strength or power used on an object.

FREEZING POINT
The temperature at which a liquid becomes a solid.

FREQUENCY
A measure (for example, in radiation) of how many waves are travel in a set time, such as a second.

FRICTION
A force that acts against motion between objects.

GRAVITY
A force that causes objects to be attracted to each other.

MAGNETIC FIELD
An area near a magnetic or electromagnetic force in which a magnet can exert magnetic force.

MAGNETISM
A process linked to electrical charge which leads to objects either being drawn toward or away from each other.

MASS
The amount of matter that any substance contains.

MOLECULE
A group of atoms bonded together.

MOMENTUM
The mass of a moving object multiplied by its velocity (speed).

PHOTOSYNTHESIS
The method that plants use to produce their own food, using sunlight to trigger a chemical reaction between carbon dioxide and water.

REFRACTION
The change in direction of a ray of light or other form of energy as it passes through some substances

STATIC ELECTRICITY
A stationary electric charge that builds up on an insulating material, as when electrons are rubbed onto wool.

THERMAL
A rising column of warm air.

VOCAL CORDS
Folds of tissue stretched across the throat, which vibrate to produce sound as air passes through them.